Newbridge Discovery Links®

How Animals Communicate

Stephen Currie

Newbridge

A Haights Cross Communications Company

How Animals Communicate
ISBN: 1-4007-3689-7

Program Author: Dr. Brenda Parkes, Literacy Expert
Content Reviewer: Eric Brothers, Biologist

Written by Stephen Currie
Design assistance by Kirchoff/Wohlberg, Inc.

Newbridge Educational Publishing
11 East 26th Street, New York, NY 10010
www.newbridgeonline.com

Cover Photograph: School of bigeye jacks
Table of Contents Photograph: Ring-tailed lemur

Photo Credits
Cover: Doug Perrine/DRK Photo; Table of Contents page: John Giustina/Bruce Coleman Inc.; page 5:
Wolfgang Bayer/Bruce Coleman Inc.; page 6: Mark J. Thomas/Dembinsky Photo Associates; page 7:
Dominique Braud/Dembinsky Photo Associates; page 8: Tom and Pat Leeson/Photo Researchers; page 9:
Roger Wilmshurst/Photo Researchers; page 10: Jen and Des Bartlett/Bruce Coleman Inc.; page 11: Danilo
Donadoni/Bruce Coleman Inc.; page 12: Mark J. Thomas/Dembinsky Photo Associates; page 14: Daniel
Zupanc/Bruce Coleman Inc.; page 15: John Cancalosi/DRK Photo; page 16: R. Mayr/OSF/Animals
Animals; page 17: E.R. Degginger/Bruce Coleman Inc., (inset) E.R. Degginger/Photo Researchers;
page 18: Joyce & Frank Burek/Animals Animals; page 19: Michael Fogden/Animals Animals; page 20:
Kenneth H. Thomas/Photo Researchers; page 21: Jerry L. Ferrara/Photo Researchers; page 22: Douglas
Faulkner/Photo Researchers; page 23: Larry Tackett/DRK Photo; page 24: Anup Shah/Animals Animals;
page 25: John C. Stevenson/Animals Animals; page 26: S. Nielsen/DRK Photo; page 27: (top) Fred
Bruemmer/DRK Photo, (bottom) Tom Bledsoe/DRK Photo; page 28: Stanley Breeden/DRK Photo;
page 29: E. Bartov/OSF/Animals Animals; page 30: F. Gohier/Photo Researchers

10 9 8 7 6 5 4 3 2 1

GUIDED READING
LEVEL **T**

Table of Contents

Staying Alive

Think of all the ways you **communicate** every day. You use words like "Hello," or "Be careful," or "I'm hungry!" Sometimes you communicate without words, by smiling or frowning or using your arm to wave to a friend.

Like humans, animals share information too. They communicate about the most important things in their world. In fact, without the ability to communicate with each other, many kinds of animals could not survive. Why is this so?

This peacock fans its huge, colorful tail to attract a mate.

Groups of howler monkeys howl loudly at the start and end of each day. Their message to other groups is: "This part of the forest is ours!" The howling can be heard several miles away.

Animals warn others in the group of danger. They direct each other to supplies of food. They send out signals to find a mate. They let other animals know that they claim a piece of land as home.

Safety. Food. Family. Home. What could be more important to an animal's survival than these things? Animals have some amazing ways of communicating. Some of the "tools" they use may surprise you!

Sending a Warning

The lives of most animals are filled with danger. They need to be on the lookout for **predators**—more powerful animals that might try to kill and eat them. For some animals, communication may be the best defense.

Most **species** of animals that live in groups send out danger warnings. Usually, if one animal senses danger, it will give an alarm signal to the rest of the group. The alarm might be a sound, a motion, or even a scent. Many animals also communicate to protect themselves. They give signals that warn predators away.

How Animals Send Danger Signals

Animal	Signal
Hog-nosed snake	Inflates its head and hisses to scare a predator. It may also play dead and release a bad scent until the predator leaves.
Bee	Releases a chemical scent when it stings to warn other bees of danger. The scent draws more bees to the attack.
Hawk moth caterpillar	Flips over to look like a snake when a predator is near
Spiny lobster	Speeds up sounds it makes to warn others of a predator
Squirrelfish	Makes noises while displaying its spiny dorsal fin to warn enemies away

The beaver uses its flat tail to steer when swimming. The tail also helps support the animal when it stands on its hind legs.

Warning Tails

Beavers sometimes use their voices to warn other beavers that a predator is around. But their most effective warning feature is probably their tails.

When a beaver senses danger, it quickly smacks its strong, paddle-shaped tail against the water. The loud sound and plume of water warn other beavers that a predator such as a mountain lion or a wolverine is near. When other beavers in the colony hear this warning sound, they dive underwater for safety.

Tails come in handy for larger animals, too. When an elephant feels threatened, it runs with its tail up. This sends a signal to others in the herd.

White-tailed deer have a special marking on their tails that serves as a signal. Deer are grazing animals, which means that they eat the grasses and other plants that grow in meadows and fields. Sometimes, they gather in herds when they're eating.

As they eat, the deer are constantly checking for predators. White-tailed deer have mostly brown fur, but underneath the tail there's a patch of white. If a deer senses danger, it turns around and leaps away. When the other deer in the herd see that flash of white, they run off too.

Here's something else to think about: Do you think the white-tailed deer is purposely warning the group by lifting its tail? Or is the deer simply running away to protect itself, incidentally showing the white spot beneath its tail?

Like the white-tailed deer, the cottontail rabbit also uses its light-colored tail as a danger signal.

As adults, most male chaffinches repeat the same song they first learned when they were young.

Red Alert!

It's easy to imagine that birds sing just for the fun of it—but that's not the only reason. Scientists called ornithologists, who study birds, know that birdcalls communicate messages. And many of their calls signal danger.

A bird called the chaffinch has three calls that sound an alarm, and each call means something different. The "whit" call is used only by male chaffinches—and only in the spring. The "tew" call is used mostly by young chaffinches. And the "seee" call is used when the danger is great.

Vervet monkeys use a range of sounds in an equally amazing way. They make different sounds to warn about different predators, such as eagles, snakes, and leopards. These sounds help other vervets in the group know exactly what they're up against!

Looking for Food

Animals must eat to stay alive, and many of them spend most of their time searching for food. Some animals hunt by themselves, but others work in groups to find the food they need. These animals need to let others in the group know what they have found, where it is, and how much of it there is.

Animals have lots of ways of communicating this important information. For example, when a scout from a colony of pine-bark beetles finds a tree to attack, it releases a chemical "messenger" called a **pheromone** from its body. Other beetles in the colony have specialized sense organs that receive the scout's message.

Gulls send out food calls to notify other gulls of a food source. However, if there's not much food to be had, a gull doesn't make a peep!

Maybe these chickens saw the food at the same moment. But more likely, one saw it first—and called the others over.

Meal Call

Chickens are great at communicating about food. If a chicken sees corn in a barnyard, it lets other chickens know about it by clucking in a certain way. Some scientists describe this food call as a "took-took-took" sound. Still, it can be hard for most people to tell the difference between this cluck and the other clucks made by chickens.

Scientists did an interesting experiment. They put one group of chickens behind a glass wall where they could be seen but not heard. A second group of chickens ignored the first group completely. Then they put a third group of chickens behind a fence where they could be heard but not seen. The second group ran toward them when they heard them clucking. What does this experiment show?

Follow the Leader

Ants don't cluck, but they have a foolproof way of telling each other where food is. If one worker ant finds some cookie crumbs on a kitchen floor, for example, it quickly returns to its nest. Before long, a string of worker ants is marching across the floor, heading directly to the crumbs.

How do they know where to go? Chemistry. Many species of ants make a trail back to the nest by releasing a pheromone that other ants can detect. All the other worker ants have to do is follow the trail in reverse to get to the food. They, too, leave pheromones along the way. If there are too many ants eating the food, or it's all gone, the last group of ants turns back without leaving a trail.

Each species of ant, such as these leaf-cutter ants, follows its own pheromone path. If a different kind of ant comes along, it will make its own trail.

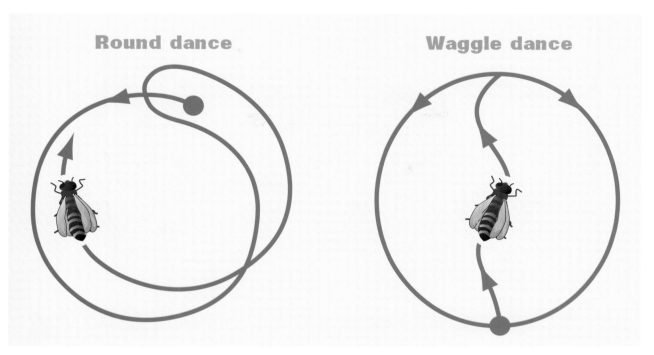

Round dance

Waggle dance

The "round dance" means food is nearby. The "waggle dance" means food is farther away. The speed and number of the bee's waggles tell how far away the food is. The direction of the waggles tells where to find the food. If the waggles go straight up toward the top of the hive, it means the bees should fly toward the sun to find the food.

In a honeybee hive, a **forager** bee that has discovered food has an interesting way of sharing the news. First, it flies back to the hive. Then it does a little dance on the wall of the honeycomb. The other bees watch carefully.

Amazingly, the forager bee's dance gives the other bees information about the location of the food. Is the bee doing its "round dance" or its "waggle dance"? That tells whether the food is near or far away. Which way did the bee move during its waggle dance? That tells the other bees which way to fly. When the dance is over, the bees hurry off to find the food, following the directions they have just been given.

Looking for a Mate

For a species to survive, new animals must be born. For this to happen, adult animals need to find mates. That gives animals another reason to communicate—courtship, or looking for a mate.

Take a look at this chart. Animals have a wide range of ways to find mates.

How Animals Find Mates

Physical Displays	Sound	Pheromones
Bower bird The male assembles twigs and leaves to form a structure called a bower to attract females. He struts and sings to entice the female into the bower.	**Red deer** The male roars and waves his antlers.	**Honeybee** The queen bee emits pheromones, sending a message that she is the only "ruler" of the hive.
Fiddler crab The male waves his claw at the female.	**Walrus** The male vocalizes to attract females.	**Hatchetfish** The female releases pheromones, which the male can smell.

This Mormon cricket is not a true cricket, but it still sings. Scientists have done experiments showing that crickets are *born* with their particular calling song. They don't have to hear other crickets to learn it.

Sing Along

Male crickets use their bodies as musical instruments. They play songs by drawing the edge of one wing against the edge of another—just as a violinist draws a bow against the strings.

The music has an important purpose. On warm nights, dozens of male crickets are out playing calling songs. With their songs, the male crickets invite females to join them. The females can tell which sounds come from males of their own species. They go in the direction of one of those sounds to find a mate.

Many birds sing, but sedge warblers are famous for their courtship songs. The males sing all day long during mating season. Their songs are very complicated. The birds almost never repeat themselves, no matter how long they sing.

The females listen to the songs. Then they choose their mates. Part of their choice has to do with the songs the males sing. How do we know? Scientists have observed that the more complicated a male warbler's song, the sooner he finds a mate.

By singing such complex songs, the male shows the female that he is healthy and strong and able to keep other birds out of the territory where he finds food. This will help the female and any offspring she and the male sedge warbler will produce.

Once a female sedge warbler joins a male, he either stops singing or hardly sings at all. The song has done its work.

Light Signals

You've probably seen fireflies flying through the air at dusk on a summer evening. From time to time, they light up. They glow for a few seconds, then turn off. Did you ever wonder what the glowing was all about?

The answer is, courtship. Just as crickets and marsh warblers use sound when they court each other, fireflies use light. They glow to show that they are looking for a mate. The male firefly will flash his light in a certain pattern. A female will flash her light in the same pattern to invite the male to land next to her.

Female fireflies of one species sometimes imitate the light pattern of a male of another species. When this "alien" male comes over, the female eats it!

Protecting Territory

Just like people, many animals mark off their own **territories** to keep others out. They have good reasons for doing this. Some animals warn intruders away from the place where they nest, or raise their babies. Others protect the areas where they find food. Still others just want to keep a little distance between themselves and the other animals that are nearby, for safety's sake.

Layers of different colors lie beneath the skin of the cuttlefish. By opening and closing pores in the skin, these creatures can change their color.

Animals have lots of ways of saying, "Keep out!" Male howler monkeys howl. Seagulls bob up and down in their nests or stand straight up to tell intruders to back off. Cuttlefish, which are related to squids, change their colors to announce, "Stay away!"

An area of land or water may be teeming with different kinds of animals. All of them have unique ways of claiming their turf.

How Animals Mark Territory

Physical Displays	Sound	Pheromones
Anole Puffs up the loose skin under its neck to look bigger and keep strangers away	**Pileated woodpecker** Drums on a hollow tree to claim a territory	**Mountain lion** Leaves its scent through its urine to mark territory
Whooping crane Struts, flaps its wings, and does a dance to scare away invaders	**Goose** Hisses and stretches its neck to chase away an enemy	**Salamander** Marks its territory with pheromones to keep out invaders

In the Water and Underground

Bullfrogs are among the world's most territorial frogs. In their crowded neighborhoods, they have to be. The ponds and streams where bullfrogs live are home to so many species of animals.

Bullfrogs have two ways of telling other bullfrogs to stay out of their space. The first is **body language.** If a bullfrog thinks another bullfrog is coming too close, it will face the newcomer and stare at it in a threatening way.

The second way involves noise and occurs during mating season. The frogs use three different signals to let others know not to come too near. Males use one, and females use another. The third is used by males and females, croaking together.

Like all frogs, the bullfrog has an eardrum on the surface of its head. Its ear is specially tuned to pick up only the noises it needs to hear. What do you think those might be?

Young prairie dogs imitating adults get so excited with jumping and yipping that they sometimes fall over backward.

Prairie dogs aren't much like bullfrogs. They're bigger, and they're **mammals,** not **amphibians.** They live in underground "towns" called burrows with hundreds of other prairie dogs. But just like bullfrogs, prairie dogs mark off territory by making a racket.

The most common prairie dog "yip" reminds intruders such as coyotes or badgers that a particular area is the prairie dog's turf. Adult prairie dogs often make this kind of territorial sound while standing up on their hind legs. If the intruder is a prairie dog from another "town," the two animals may nip, sniff, and charge at each other, but not to cause harm. They do this to establish who's in control.

Staying Together

Many animal species live in groups. Their families feed together, nest together, travel together, and protect each other. The mothers, and sometimes the fathers, help raise and teach the offspring.

These animals have developed different ways to stay together. Most of these ways involve communication about danger, food, mating, and territory. But they also communicate with others in their group through touch. Animal groups can be found in the sea, on land, and in the air.

Manatees often nuzzle each other's snouts when they meet underwater.

Fish use visual clues to stay together. Since their eyes are located at the sides of their head, they can detect a wide range of movement going on around them.

Fish are among the most visible of these animals. Many types of fish, such as sardines, herring, anchovies, and mackerel, swim in groups called schools. Some schools can stretch for miles and include hundreds of fish.

What's the benefit of being in a school? It's that all those fish together look much more powerful than a few swimming alone. When predators see the large group, they tend to stay away!

How do fish stay in their school? Each fish gets information from the fish in front of it. For example, when one fish changes direction, the one behind follows it. In an amazingly few seconds, the message gets passed along from the first fish to the ones at the back of the school. Safety in numbers helps them to survive.

On land, many species of animals also stick together. Chimpanzees live in groups. They search for food together. And when they find it, they notify other chimps by screaming, hitting logs, and hooting! Often they play games together, which not all animals do.

One thing that helps chimps **bond** to one another within their group is touch. Chimpanzees kiss each other and slap one another on the back, just as humans do. Chimps also groom each other's fur. They pick out bugs and smooth the fur. This pleasurable behavior helps keep the group together.

These chimps are grooming each other. All this touching lets other chimps know that they are important members of the group.

The "language" of Canada geese contains at least ten different honking sounds.

One group of birds that you may have seen are Canada geese. But you probably *heard* them before you saw them soaring through the air! That's because these birds make loud "honk–honk–honk" sounds as they migrate from Canada to the warmer climates of the southern United States and Mexico for the winter. What's all the noise about?

These migrating birds honk constantly to urge each other on. Canada geese fly great distances at speeds as fast as 60 miles per hour, so they probably appreciate the support!

Early Learners

How do animals get so good at communicating? Are these skills **innate,** which means the animals are born with them? Or do parents teach their young? In the animal world, there is more than one answer to those questions. But one thing is sure—mother animals and their babies keep the lines of communication open!

Mallard ducks often make little noises at their eggs—and the chicks inside the eggs actually answer back. What are they saying? Some scientists think that the chicks are just getting used to their mother's voice. This may prepare the ducklings to bond with her for safety once they are born. Other scientists think the pre-birth "conversations" help the ducklings figure out when to hatch so they all hatch around the same time.

Mother bats use scent to find their babies, but they also use sound. Since bats live together in huge groups, you might think it would be hard to know who's talking! But in a cave filled with thousands of bat mothers and young, or pups, each mother can recognize the cry of her pup, and each pup knows its mom's special cry.

Mother bears teach their young important survival skills by showing them exactly what to do. For example, the cub gets a lesson in catching fish by seeing how its mother finds them.

Learning More About Animals

Nature has provided animals with many tools for communication—and there are probably more that we don't even know of yet. As animal scientists continue to explore this fascinating area, we will learn more.

For several years, scientists have been exploring a kind of communication that's very effective, yet requires no fancy displays or loud calls or pheromones. Instead, animals use vibration to send their messages. It's called **bioseismics,** and is common among **rodents.**

This wallaby, which lives in Australia, drums with its foot when it senses danger.

The Palestine mole rat also uses its head as a shovel to dig tunnels underground. It uses its nose, which has a hard covering to protect it, to pack the dirt walls of the tunnel.

For example, a kangaroo rat that lives alone underground will thump its large foot on the ground very fast to tell others, "This is my space." A giant kangaroo rat can thump its foot on the ground 18 times a second. The foot-drumming causes the ground to vibrate. And when the other kangaroo rats feel the vibes, they get the message!

Mole rats use head-drumming to establish their territory. These animals also use sound and smell to communicate with each other in the tunnels they dig underground. One animal, the European mole vole, drums on the ground with its front teeth!

Bioseismics is a fairly new area of study for scientists, and there is more to discover about this interesting form of animal communication. But often, animals that people have studied for years and years still hold some mystery.

For example, male humpback whales sing complicated songs during mating season. Scientists have been studying these songs for a long time, but they are still finding out new information about the messages the songs contain.

There is still much to be learned about the way animals communicate, but you don't have to be a scientist to study this fascinating topic. You can explore animal communication too. Find an animal to check out. Look at its body language. Listen to the sounds it makes. What do you think it is saying? How do you think its communication helps it survive?

The whale songs are so beautiful that people buy recordings of them to enjoy as music.

Glossary

amphibian: an animal such as a frog, toad, or salamander that spends part of its life under water and part on land

bioseismics: a kind of communication in which animals send messages to each other through vibrations in the ground. They use their feet, heads, or teeth to produce the vibrations.

body language: a way of communicating that uses physical movements to express feelings or ideas, such as cringing to show fear

bond: form a close relationship

communicate: express ideas or feelings to others

forager: an animal that searches for food

innate: possessed from birth. Innate behavior is based on knowledge that an animal is born with.

mammal: an animal such as a bear, horse, dog, or cat that has hair and produces milk to feed its young

pheromone: a chemical substance that some animals emit, or give off, to communicate information. Other animals of the same species can smell the pheromone or detect it in other ways.

predator: an animal that hunts and eats other animals for food

rodent: a small mammal with sharp front teeth that are good for gnawing food and other things. Some rodents are squirrels, chipmunks, rats, mice, and voles.

species: a particular kind of living thing. Animals of the same species look alike and are similar in other ways.

territory: an area of land inhabited by one or more animals that includes places where they can find food and raise their young

Index

Website

To learn more about animals and how they communicate,
visit this Website:

www.fonz.org/animals.htm